Lord, make me an instrument of Your peace. Where there is hatred, let me sow love; Where there is injury, pardon; Where there is doubt, faith; Where there is despair, hope; Where there is sadness, joy.

O Divine Master, grant that I may not so much seek to be consoled as to console; To be understood as to understand; To be loved as to love; For it is in giving that we receive; It is in pardoning that we are pardoned; And it is in dying that we are born to eternal life.

Prayer for Peace of Saint Francis of Assisi - One of Mother Teresa's Special Prayers

For Sam Eagle - A.D

First published in Great Britain in 1999 by Element Children's Books
Shaftesbury, Dorset SP7 8BP

Published in the USA in 2000 by Element Books, Inc.
160 North Washington Street, Boston MA 02114
First published in paperback in 1999

Published in Australia in 1999 by Element Books
and distributed by Penguin Australia Limited
487 Maroondah Highway, Ringwood, Victoria 3134

Cover and text illustrations © Allan Drummond
Cover and text design by Dominic Owen

Printed and bound by Colorcraft in Hong Kong

British Library Cataloguing in Publication data available.
Library of Congress Cataloging in Publication data available.

ISBN 1 902618 65 3 HB
ISBN 1 902618 31 9 PB

Publisher's note:
This book uses American English spelling and punctuation.

STORIES TOLD BY

MOTHER TERESA

Compiled by Edward Le Joly & Jaya Chaliha
ABRIDGED AND ILLUSTRATED BY ALLAN DRUMMOND

ELEMENT
CHILDREN'S BOOKS

SHAFTESBURY, DORSET · BOSTON, MASSACHUSETTS · MELBOURNE, VICTORIA

Children were very, very special to Mother Teresa. Her smiling wrinkled face and bright blue eyes radiated love as she stretched out her big work-worn hands to welcome them. Mother Teresa was once a plump little girl, neat and tidy and ever ready to lend a helping hand. She was born in Skopje, now the capital of Macedonia, in 1910. Her name was Agnes Gonxha Bojaxhiu. At home she was called Gonxha which in Albanian means a flower bud. Her older sister and brother were Age and Lazar. When Mother Teresa was presented with the Nobel Peace Prize in Oslo in 1979, Lazar said that his little sister was always "sensible and serious" and that when she caught him stealing the jam, she would scold him but never carried tales.

Agnes was very close to her mother, Roza. Her father Nikola died when she was seven years old and the family were not as well-off as they had been before. Roza continued to give money and food to the poor and Agnes would often accompany her and say, "She taught us to love God and our neighbor."

The Bojaxhiu family lived in a house with a garden near the big Roman Catholic church. The children attended services here with their mother. Agnes would lead the choir with her beautiful soprano voice.

At Sunday school, she would listen wide-eyed to talks about priests and nuns working among the people, and especially the children, in India. She felt a "call" deep inside her to become a nun and work in India.

When Agnes was eighteen years old, she left her home to join the Congregation (Order) of Loreto nuns in Dublin, Ireland. She learnt English in a very short time and was soon on her way to India. She completed her training (noviciate) and took the name Teresa in 1931.

The young Sister Teresa also learnt Bengali and Hindi and began teaching in the Loreto schools. She was later headmistress of St.Mary's school in Calcutta.

In 1946, Mother was traveling by train to Darjeeling, when she received another "call" to work with the "poorest of the poor" and was again sure that the "call" was from God. This was the biggest step in her life and she had to prepare herself as quickly as possible. Alone she began her new work in the slums near her old school and on the streets of Calcutta.

The news of her wonderful work quickly spread and the Congregation of the Missionaries of Charity (MCs) – Mother Teresa's order – was blessed by the Pope in 1950. The first to join her were two of her own students from St.Mary's. The work of Mother Teresa and her Sisters became known outside India and she was asked to open homes for the poor and homeless in other countries. She did so and the list keeps growing. There are now Brothers and Sisters from India and from all over the world working in more than 600 homes and in 136 countries.

The lifestyle of the MCs is very simple with just the basic necessities. Mother's day began at 4.30 a.m. and she worked and prayed the whole day till late into the night.

Mother never wrote down her speeches or talks. The stories related in this book are about

"the little things of everyday life." They are Mother Teresa's own personal experience and she used them to illustrate her message; touching the hearts and minds of millions.

As the work of the MCs spread, so did the name of their founder, Mother Teresa. She received so many awards and honorary degrees from so many nations and well-known universities that Mother lost count of them. Mother did not like the publicity and said, "I receive them in the name of the poor."

Mother handed over the running of the MCs and blessed her successor, Sister Nirmala, before she died on 5 September 1997. She is buried in Mother House, Calcutta. At examination time, children from all over the city come in hundreds to place a flower on Mother's simple snow white tomb, and ask for her blessing.

The small wooden board outside the door to Mother House reads "Mother Teresa." The IN and OUT indicator is fixed. Mother is always IN.

JAYA CHALIHA

The Runaway

FOR many children in the city of Calcutta the street is their only home. One evening Mother Teresa found a little boy sitting on the ground in the busy road where she lived. She bent down to talk to him, and seeing that he was all alone she asked one of the Sisters to take him to the childrens' home. The boy smiled with delight as the Sisters gave him a bath and fresh clean clothes before putting him to bed.

The next day Mother Teresa passed by and asked the Sisters about him. "Oh dear!" they cried, "He ran away in the middle of the night." So a search was begun in the noisy, crowded streets and quite soon the boy was found. But the next night he ran away again. Luckily, when day came, he was found wandering about in the heat and dust. So Mother Teresa said, "If he runs away again, please follow him and see where he goes." Sure enough, that night he disappeared again. And this time a Sister found him crouching in the dark by a little fire. He was with a woman who was cooking leftovers of food she had found on the ground.

"Why did you run away from our home?" the Sister asked the child. The boy explained that the woman beside him was his mother. *"This is my home* because this is where my mother is!" he said smiling. He had no shelter, but he had his mother, and that was home.

Once there was a shortage of sugar in Calcutta and this lack of sugar became a crisis for the Sisters working with Mother Teresa because it was a basic food for the children. The Sisters, who worked all over the city would go to Mother Teresa saying,

"There is no sugar for the children."

Mother Teresa

On one very busy day at the home everyone was worrying about the sugar crisis. The subject became so big it was difficult to think of anything else until suddenly Mother Teresa spotted a little boy looking up into her face and smiling. He had come out of curiosity to look at the famous Mother Teresa. She smiled back and put her arms around the child, and explaining why she had not noticed him before said,

"Mother Teresa has no sugar for her children." The boy thought about this on his way home and told his family in great excitement that he had met Mother Teresa. "I will not eat sugar for three days. I will give my sugar to Mother Teresa," he announced. Sure enough, a few days later the boy led his parents to Mother's house.

has no sugar

As soon as he saw Mother Teresa coming he smiled and held out the sugar he had saved up. And after that Mother Teresa would often say ...

"That little boy was so young he could hardly say my name but he loved with great love.

He taught me that it is not how much we give, but *how much love we put in that giving* that is important."

Professor...

AFTER the success of her mission in Calcutta, Mother Teresa went to Venezuela in South America to open her first mission outside India.

A new home for orphaned children was to be built, and the people who had given the plot of land for it were a rich family who lived nearby. So one day she went to visit them.

As she went into their house she was greeted cheerfully by the mother of the family who introduced Mother Teresa to her oldest child.

"What is his name?" Mother Teresa asked, because she could see that the boy was very disabled, and she guessed that he could not speak.

"His name is Professor of Love ..." the mother replied, laughing.

Mother Teresa noticed the beautiful smile on the mother's face as she said these words, "... because this child is teaching us the whole time how to express *love in action.*"

...of love

IF you were one of the many people who went to Mother Teresa asking, "How can I help the poorest of the poor?" you might have been surprised at her answer. *"I want you to find the poor,* right in your own home first. And begin love there.

The courage

Find out about the people who live next door – do you know who they are?"

She told this extraordinary story about a very poor family who showed love to their neighbors ... "A man came to our house and said, 'Mother Teresa there is a family with eight children who have not eaten for some time. Please do something for them.' So I took some rice and went there immediately.

And I saw the children — their eyes shining with hunger. Their mother took the rice from me, divided it into two and then started to walk out of her house with the other half. 'Where are you going?' I cried. 'They are hungry also,' was all she said, and then she left. When she came back she

to give

explained that her neighbors were hungry too. She had given half of the rice to them.

Now what really surprised me was not that she gave, but that she knew her next door neighbors were hungry, for usually when we are suffering or in trouble we have no time for others. But this mother had the *courage of her love to give.*"

wants me

In cities all over the world there are people sleeping in the streets. There is poverty in Calcutta, but there is also poverty in the rich cities of America and Europe. It is said that about five thousand people sleep in the streets of San Francisco at night.

When Mother Teresa spoke about poverty to helpers in these rich countries, she would often talk about another kind of poverty – *poverty of the spirit.*

Yes, the homeless sleep on the streets at night, she would say, but there is another kind of homelessness which we must all think about.

And she went on to talk about the homelessness of being unwanted, unloved and uncared for.

"We live in a throw-away society," she said. "We throw things away when they do not work properly or when they are empty. People and families too easily reject one another, and we have so many people who have been thrown away."

"I will never forget a little child who came knocking on our door around midnight, crying at the top of his voice and saying, 'I went to my father, my father didn't want me. I went to my mother, my mother didn't want me. Do you want me?'

"Naturally I wanted him very much, for that little one was so hurt."

ONCE there was a woman who was so impressed by what Mother Teresa was saying that she immediately took off her gold bangles and offered them as gifts.

But Mother Teresa did not take them. Instead she told this story ... "A rich man came to me and said, 'I have a big house in Holland. Do you want me to give it up?' I said 'No.' 'Do you want me to live in that house?' he suggested.

Helping, Mother

'Yes.' I said. 'I have a big car, do you want me to give that up instead?' he replied.

'No, but what I want you to do is go back and see lonely people who live in Holland. Then, every now and then I want you to bring a few at a time and entertain them. Bring them in that car of yours and let them enjoy a few hours in your beautiful house. Then your big house will become a place of love –

13

full of light, full of joy, full of life.'

He smiled and said he would be so happy to bring the people to his home, but that he wanted to give up something in his life. So I suggested, 'When you go to the store to buy a new suit or clothes, instead of buying the best, buy something cheaper and use that extra money to buy something for somebody else, or better still for the poor.'

"When I finished he looked amazed and exclaimed, 'Oh! Is that the way, Mother? I never thought of it.'"

Teresa's way

CAN you imagine what the pain of real hunger is like? For those of us who have never been really starving it is impossible to imagine.

Mother Teresa spent a lifetime working amongst the hungry, and she told this story about a little child she picked up in the street.

Mother Teresa first told this story to a group of her friends and followers. These people had never felt hunger for food, but she guessed that they had probably suffered the hunger for love.

The hunger for love is something we all feel.

Open your eyes

"He was just six years old. I could see from his eyes that he was very, very hungry. I have seen that terrible hunger in many eyes. I gave him a piece of bread and instead of eating it as fast as possible, he started eating it crumb by crumb. I said to him, 'Eat the bread, you are hungry.' And that little one looked at me and said; 'I am afraid that the bread will be finished and I will be hungry again.'"

This important lesson Mother Teresa learned during her time working with the poor. She told her friends ... "That little one already knows the pain of hunger you and I may not know. That is why I say: Open your eyes and see, for there is hunger not only for a piece of bread; there is hunger for understanding, love, and for the word of God."

smartly dressed in matching shirts and caps given to them by the airline. These were some of Calcutta's poorest children who had never even left their street, let alone their city.

"And now we will be soaring high above it!" announced a little boy as they clambered into their

Christmas and

EVERY Christmas Mother Teresa would write a letter to her helpers with happy greetings and a special message.

One Christmas she wrote with delight of how 150 children from her homes were amazed to hear that they would be given an extra special present – a free ride in an airplane!

The children gathered at the airport, all

seats and fastened their seatbelts.

Woosh! The speed of the take-off sent a thrill through the children, and once the plane was flying smoothly they were allowed to get out of their seats and look through the windows and wonder at the city they had left so far below.

Then the time to land came all too quickly. The huge and busy city they had left behind, with its crowded streets, seemed to rush up to meet them. And everyone cheered as the wheels of the airplane touched the ground.

Mother Teresa wrote about the joy of those abandoned children who had been lifted out of their day to day lives by the special flight.

the family

"How wonderful that our abandoned, handicapped, hungry children were given the chance ... to experience the joy of flying," Mother Teresa said in her letter. But as if coming down to earth, the rest of her Christmas message was about how, here on the ground, the best place for children to learn to love and pray is in the family.

"When families are strong and united, children can see God's special love in the *love of their father and mother...*"

Prizes for

ONE afternoon a small group of schoolchildren gathered at the doorway of the Mother House. "Does Mother Teresa live here?" they all asked.

the Poor

So Mother Teresa was called, and although she was busy with a group of visitors she came to the door and saw straight away that the children had come with their headmistress on a special mission. Two children stepped forward and explained why they had come.

"We came first and second in our classes this year and we were supposed to be presented with gifts on prize giving day," announced the first child.

"But the day before prize giving we asked for money instead," said the other. Mother Teresa was curious. "Why money?" she asked.

"Well, on prize giving day we said, 'Take us to Mother Teresa, *we want to give this money to her poor people,'* they explained. Then they handed the envelopes to Mother Teresa, smiled proudly and everyone clapped their hands in joy.

When they had gone, Mother Teresa returned to her visitors and said, "Now see how wonderful it was that they didn't use the money for themselves. Whenever I accept money or an award or anything, I always take it in the name of the poor who they see in me. I think I am right because, after all, who am I? I am nothing. Because they see, they believe."

Prince Charles

KINGS, presidents, and many famous people have cuddled and cradled the children and babies in Mother Teresa's special homes all over the world.

Once Prince Charles visited Calcutta, and found time to go to the home where he met Mother Teresa.

Straight away she introduced him to the newest member of her family – a tiny crying baby who had been abandoned somewhere in the city, and the Prince smiled as he held the little child.

Next Mother Teresa took the Prince to the chapel where they prayed quietly together. And after this she gave him the gift of a little card with the famous prayer by St. Francis of Assisi printed on it which begins ... "Lord make me an instrument of thy peace ..."

She asked the Prince to say the prayer every day, and he told Mother Teresa how impressed he was by the work at the home.

Then as he was about to leave she turned to him and said ... "I cannot do what you do, and you cannot do what I can do, but together *the two of us can do something beautiful for God."*

A priest who went every morning to one of the high schools in Sahebganga always took his big friendly dog with him, but the Mother Superior would never allow it to enter the house.

That was until the day Mother Teresa came to celebrate the school's 25th anniversary.

"Mother Teresa is coming to make a speech at the jubilee!" the children cried. There was great excitement and so many people came to see Mother that it soon became clear that the school hall was not going to be big enough. Finally everyone gathered in the park nearby to hear her, and later she went back into the school to have tea with the Sisters.

Animal lover

The priest and his dog followed the crowd back to the school and the Sisters invited him to join them in the house. The dog was left outside as usual but during tea the dog sneaked in as the door was opened. The Sister Superior got up to chase the great animal out, "Shoo!" But Mother Teresa immediately exclaimed, "What a nice dog," and held it in her arms and stroked it and kissed it.

There was laughter all round,

and the big friendly dog remained close to her as the school celebrations continued.

And from the next morning onwards the dog was always allowed in the house. Everyone loved it because Mother Teresa had blessed it.